ANIMALS OF THE SERENGETI
Wildlife of East Africa
Encyclopedias for Children

SPEEDY
PUBLISHING

The Serengeti is a region of savannah in East Africa.

Elephants are the largest land-living mammal in the world.

Elephants are herbivores meaning they only eat plants and vegetables. Elephants travel in a herd lead by a female.

Lions are the second largest big cat species in the world.

Lion's are
known as king
of the jungle,
but they really
don't live
in jungles.

Hippopotamuses are a semi-aquatic animal meaning they spend a lot of the time in the water.

They are
regarded
as one of
the most
dangerous
animals in
Africa.

Zebras are members of the horse family. Every zebra has a unique pattern of black and white stripes.

When zebras
are grouped
together, their
stripes make
it hard for a
lion or leopard
to pick out
one zebra
to chase.

Giraffes are
the tallest
land animals.
A giraffe can
live 25 years
in the wild and
30 in captivity.

Giraffes eat leaves and branches mostly from acacia, mimosa and wild apricot trees.

African buffalo is a large animal that can reach 6.8 to 11 feet in length and weigh between 660 and 1900 pounds.

African buffalo has poor eyesight and sense of hearing, but their sense of smell is excellent.

**Wildebeest
is a mammal
that belongs
to the family
of antelopes.**

During migration, wildebeests travel between 500 and 1000 miles.

Hyenas are large, dog-like, carnivores. Hyenas use various sounds, postures and signals to communicate with each other.

Hyenas live in territorial and large clans that can consist of up to 80 members.

Cheetah's are
the fastest
land mammal
in the world.
They can run
at speeds up
to 75 miles
per hour.

Cheetah's do not roar like lions or tigers. They let out a chirping noise when they feel threatened.

Visit
BABY PROFESSOR
EDUCATION KIDS
www.BabyProfessorBooks.com
to download Free Baby Professor eBooks
and view our catalog of new and exciting
Children's Books